McLEAN MERCER REGIONAL LIBRARY
BOX 505
RIVERDALE, ND 58565

DRAGONS

by Carla Mooney

Content Consultant
Joseph Nigg
Author of *Wonder Beasts*
and other books on mythical animals

CORE
LIBRARY

Published by ABDO Publishing Company, PO Box 398166, Minneapolis, MN 55439. Copyright © 2014 by Abdo Consulting Group, Inc. International copyrights reserved in all countries. No part of this book may be reproduced in any form without written permission from the publisher. The Core Library™ is a trademark and logo of ABDO Publishing Company.

Printed in the United States of America,
North Mankato, Minnesota
092013
012014

♻ THIS BOOK CONTAINS AT LEAST 10% RECYCLED MATERIALS.

Editor: Lauren Coss
Series Designer: Becky Daum

Library of Congress Cataloging-in-Publication Data
Mooney, Carla, 1970-
  Dragons / by Carla Mooney.
      pages cm. -- (Creatures of legend)
  Includes index.
  ISBN 978-1-62403-151-9
1. Dragons. I. Title.
  GR830.D7M668 2014
  398.24'54--dc23
                                    2013026941

Photo Credits: Thinkstock, cover, 1, 10, 16, 21, 24, 32 (left), 42 (top), 42 (bottom); Ivy Close Images/Alamy, 4; North Wind/North Wind Picture Archives, 7, 27, 28; Shutterstock Images, 13, 32 (right), 41; Geoff Hardy/ Shutterstock Images, 19; Ivy Close Images/Alamy, 30; Red Line Editorial, 32 (main), 43; DreamWorks SKG/Everett Collection, 34, 45; Warner Brothers/ Everett Collection, 37; 20th Century Fox Film Corp./Everett Collection, 39

CONTENTS

CHAPTER ONE

THE LEGENDARY DRAGON

A dreadful dragon threatened King Beowulf's land. Each night, the dragon terrorized the countryside. It breathed fire over houses, farms, and fields. King Beowulf wondered why the dragon had come to his land. Finally, one of the king's servants confessed. He had stolen a jeweled cup from the dragon's lair. The dragon had begun its attacks the night after the cup was stolen.

The story of Beowulf and the dragon is one of the oldest written dragon legends.

Battling the Dragon

King Beowulf was determined to save his kingdom. He gathered a group of men. But most of the men ran away in fear when they reached the dragon's lair. Only Beowulf's loyal friend Wiglaf stayed to fight.

Beowulf bravely climbed into the cave's opening. He shouted a challenge to the monster. The sleeping dragon awoke. It shot a stream of fire from its jaws. Then it raced toward Beowulf.

Beowulf held an iron shield to protect himself from the dragon's fiery breath. The king struck the dragon with his sword. The sword bounced off the dragon's tough scales. The dragon came in for a second attack. This time Wiglaf stepped forward

A 1,000-year-old page from a *Beowulf* manuscript can be found in the British Library in London, England.

to help the king. The dragon's fire burned Wiglaf's wooden shield. Wiglaf huddled with Beowulf under the king's iron shield. Again, Beowulf struck the dragon. This time his sword shattered on the dragon's skull.

The dragon attacked a third time. It bit Beowulf's neck with its sharp fangs. Blood gushed from Beowulf's wound. Wiglaf rushed to save his king. Scales did not protect the dragon's belly. Wiglaf drove a giant sword through the monster's belly and into

One Weakness

In many stories, including *Beowulf*, there is a small part of the dragon's belly not protected by scales. According to a Scandinavian legend, a dragon named Fafnir guarded a gold treasure in his cave. A dwarf named Regin wanted Fafnir's gold. Regin convinced Sigurd, a young knight, to attack the dragon. Fafnir's belly was vulnerable. Sigurd dug a deep pit in the ground. He hid inside the pit and waited. When the dragon crawled across the pit, Sigurd thrust his sword into the dragon's belly. He killed the dragon.

its heart. Then Beowulf stabbed the dragon's belly with a battle knife. Finally, the dragon fell. But the dragon had seriously wounded the king. Dragon poison quickly spread through his body. The old king died. However, his kingdom was at last free from the terror of the dragon.

Dragon Myths

People have told stories about dragons for thousands of years. The story of Beowulf is based on a long poem written in England around 700 CE. At one time, many people thought dragons were real. Today we know dragons are mythical.

In this passage from *Beowulf*, the poet describes the dragon's attack on Beowulf's kingdom. The poet calls the dragon "the stranger" and "the enemy":

> The stranger began then to vomit forth fire,
>
> To burn the great manor; the blaze then glimmered
>
> For anguish to earlmen, not anything living
>
> Was the hateful air-goer willing to leave there.
>
> The war of the worm widely was noticed,
>
> The feud of the foeman afar and anear,
>
> How the enemy injured the earls of the Geatmen,
>
> Harried with hatred: back he hied to the treasure,
>
> To the well-hidden cavern ere the coming of daylight.
>
> He had circled with fire the folk of those regions,
>
> With brand and burning; in the barrow he trusted,

Source: Beowulf. *Trans. Lesslie Hall. Boston: D.C. Heath and Co., 1892. p. 79.* Project Gutenberg. *Web. Accessed July 30, 2013.*

Consider Your Audience

Beowulf contains many words no longer used today. Ask an adult to help you figure out any words that are unfamiliar to you. What is the poet trying to describe? Rewrite this passage for a modern audience.

CHAPTER TWO

PORTRAIT OF A DRAGON

I n many stories, the dragon is described as a giant reptile-like creature. The dragon is often a feared fighter. Its body is built for battle. Dragons often attack from the air. They swoop down on animals and people.

Fiery breath is one of the dragon's most dangerous weapons. In many legends, dragons blast fire from their mouths. They can burn objects

Dragons come in many different shapes and sizes.

hundreds of yards away. Some dragons also blow poisonous smoke from their mouths.

Dragons usually have scales from head to toe. Scales protect their bodies from attacks. However, the dragon's belly is often not protected by scales.

Dragon Magic

Many dragons have magical powers. In some stories, dragons can read minds. Other dragons can shape-shift to change the way they look. In some legends, dragons can paralyze people by looking them in the eyes.

In other stories, dragons get their powers from magical objects. The objects may be jewels the dragon wears. For example, the Asian *lung* gets its powers from a magical pearl it carries.

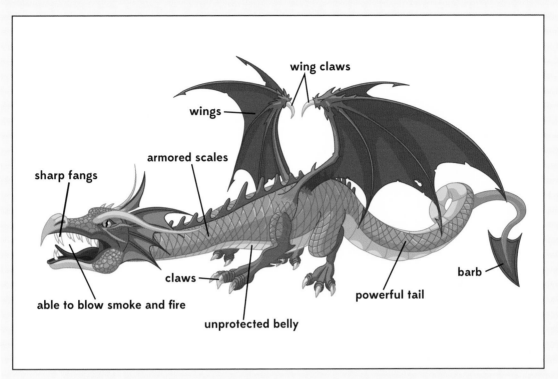

Dragon Anatomy
This graphic shows the powerful body of a dragon. After reading about dragons, how did you imagine their bodies would look? What features shown here might help this dragon in battle?

A Dragon's Life

According to different legends, dragons can live almost anywhere. In some Asian legends, dragons swim to underwater caves at the bottom of oceans, lakes, and rivers. In most stories, dragons live alone. Many choose a hidden lair as a safe place to rest.

In many myths, dragons collect treasure. The treasure can include gold coins, silver cups, or colored gems. Some dragons collect magical objects, such as enchanted swords or charmed rings. Dragons store their treasure in their lairs. They often guard the treasure fiercely.

Stealing its treasure is a surefire way to make a dragon mad. In one ancient Greek myth, a hero named Jason travels to the island of Colchis. To regain his lost throne, he must steal the Golden Fleece. The Golden Fleece is the fleece of a golden ram that has magical healing

Magical Healing Powers

In the past, some people believed dragon parts had magical or healing powers. The Chinese believed powdered dragon bones were a cure for many illnesses. The bones they thought came from dragons were often dinosaur bones. In the West, people believed spreading dragon blood over a person's skin would protect the person from all types of wounds. The "dragon's blood" was actually sap from plants and trees.

EXPLORE ONLINE

Chapter Two discusses the dragon's appearance and behavior. It also tells the story of Jason and the Golden Fleece. The Web site at the link below also discusses the Jason legend. As you know, every source is different. How is the information on the Web site different from the information in this chapter? What information is the same? How do the two sources present information differently? What can you learn from this Web site?

Jason and the Golden Fleece
www.mycorelibrary.com/dragons

powers. But a fierce dragon guards the fleece. Jason finds the place where the fleece is hidden. He uses a magic potion to lull the dragon to sleep. Then he kills the dragon and takes the Golden Fleece.

The story of Jason is more than 2,000 years old. But some legends about dragons are even older.

CHAPTER THREE

THE MYTH'S BEGINNINGS

Stories about dragons exist all over the world. Some legends are more than 4,000 years old. In the past, people often made up stories to explain events or things they did not understand. Dragon legends may have started from the stories ancient people told to explain strange or unfamiliar animals.

Through the 1700s, many people believed dragons were real creatures. Today most people know dragons are mythical.

Dinosaurs

In many ways, dinosaurs look like the legendary dragons. Many dinosaurs were huge and powerful. They protected themselves with sharp teeth and tough, armor-like skin. Tyrannosaurus rex (T. rex) was one of the largest dinosaurs. It grew up to 40 feet (12 m) long. A T. rex could be 15 to 20 feet (4.6–6 m) tall. It moved quickly with its strong legs. The T. rex also had a powerful tail. Its sharp, knife-like teeth could easily rip its prey's flesh.

Pterosaurs were winged reptiles that also lived during the dinosaur age. They were very similar to

In the past, people may have mistaken the skeletons of dinosaurs, such as the T. rex, for the remains of dragons.

dragons. Like dragons, pterosaurs swooped from the sky to grab their prey.

T. rex and pterosaur fossils have been found on several continents. Ancient humans likely could not

19

Eyewitnesses

Sometimes legends begin when people report an animal they saw with their own eyes. In the 400s BCE, Greek scholar Herodotus traveled to Egypt and Arabia. There he claimed to see skeletons of winged, snake-like creatures. In the late 1200s CE, explorer Marco Polo reported seeing dragons in China. Some historians believe these eyewitnesses may have seen real, but unfamiliar animals. Without photographs, descriptions changed over time. Eventually the unknown animals became dragons.

have imagined an animal with such enormous bones. Historians believe these people may have created dragon stories to explain the bones.

Reptiles

Reptiles share many traits with dragons. Crocodiles, alligators, and giant lizards have scaly skin, large teeth, and powerful tails. As people saw these terrifying animals, they told stories about them. Over time, storytellers may have added new details. The animals grew wings and breathed fire. They became dragons.

Monitor lizards are similar to dragons. In fact they are some of the most dangerous lizards alive today.

The Komodo dragon is a species of monitor lizard that lives in Indonesia. Komodo dragons can grow up to 10 feet (3 m) long.

Monitor lizards live in Africa, Asia, and Australia. These reptiles have long, strong tails and razor-sharp claws. Monitor lizards can climb and swim easily. They hiss to scare prey. The lizards often rise on their hind legs before attacking. Like dragons, monitor lizards can deliver deadly blows with their tails. Some monitor lizards have even been known to attack and kill humans.

Ocean Animals

Some dragon legends may have come from sightings of ocean animals. While crossing oceans, ancient sailors may have caught quick glimpses of large whales, giant squid, or sharks. Wondering what these animals were, they may have called them dragons. Large bones and skeletons from these ocean animals may have been strange to ancient people. They might not have known the bones came from a sea creature. Dragon stories would help explain such finds.

Birds

Certain large birds may have also been confused with dragons in ancient times. Birds of prey, such as eagles, vultures, and falcons, hunt from the air. Soaring overhead, they may have looked like dragons to ancient people. While no one is certain how the legend first started, myths about dragons can be found all over the world.

Explorer Marco Polo traveled to Asia from 1271 to 1295 CE. When he returned, he described firsthand encounters with enormous serpents:

> *You may be assured that some of them are ten paces in length; some are more and some less. And in bulk they are equal to a great cask, for the bigger ones are about ten palms in girth. They have two forelegs near the head, but for foot nothing but a claw like the claw of a hawk or that of a lion. The head is very big, and the eyes are bigger than a great loaf of bread. The mouth is large enough to swallow a man whole, and is garnished with great [pointed] teeth. And in short they are so fierce-looking and so hideously ugly, that every man and beast must stand in fear and trembling of them. There are also smaller ones, such as of eight paces long, and of five, and of one pace only.*

Source: Marco Polo and Rustichello of Pisa. The Travels of Marco Polo, Volume 2. Trans. Henry Yule. Ed. Henri Cordier. n.p., 1903. Project Gutenberg. *Web.* Accessed July 30, 2013.

Changing Minds

Some people believe Polo only saw a crocodile. What do you think? Take a position on what creature he saw. Then imagine your best friend has the opposite opinion. Write a short essay trying to change your friend's mind. Make sure you explain your opinion and your reasons for it.

CHAPTER FOUR

FEARED FIGHTER OR GENTLE GIANT?

Almost every culture has a story about dragons. In legends from the West and the East, dragons are very different creatures. The Western legends mainly come from Europe. The Eastern legends come from Asia. In Western legends, dragons can be deadly monsters. In Eastern legends, most dragons are kind helpers.

Eastern dragons are very different from the dragons of European cultures.

The Legend of Apep

Some dragon legends helped explain nature. Ancient Egyptians may have used the legend of Apep to explain why the sun was blacked out during what is now known as a solar eclipse. In ancient Egypt, the god Apep was a huge dragon-like monster. He wanted to devour the sun. Each night after the sun set, the sun god, Ra, sailed a great solar ship through the underworld. Each day, as dawn neared and Ra returned with the sun from the underworld, Apep attacked. Sometimes Apep swallowed the solar ship whole. But the gods were able to cut the solar ship from his belly. They returned the ship to the sky.

The Western Dragon: A Deadly Enemy

Dragons in Western stories are often dangerous. Many dragons live in caves. Some of these dragons guard treasure. When hungry, they snatch sheep, cattle, and even humans. The Western dragon is a fearsome sight. It is scaly and serpent-like. It has legs, wings, and a barbed tail. It breathes fire and soars across the sky.

In Christian tales, dragons often represent sin or the devil.

Saint George and the Dragon

Saint George is believed to be a real soldier who lived in the 300s CE. Although little is known about his life, there are many legends surrounding him. In one famous tale from the Middle Ages in Europe, Saint George battles a dragon to save a princess.

Saint George is one of the most famous dragon killers of legend.

According to the legend, a huge, winged dragon lived in a lake near Silene, Libya. The dragon terrorized Silene. It killed and ate anyone it saw. To keep the dragon happy, the villagers offered it sacrifices of sheep. When they ran out of sheep, they sacrificed the king's daughter. They tied the princess to a wooden stake at the edge of the lake.

Saint George promised to save the princess and defeat the dragon. When the dragon came out of the lake, George charged at it on his horse. He thrust his lance at the dragon. George pierced the dragon's throat and pinned it to the ground. Then George tied the wounded dragon to a leash. He and the princess led the dragon back to the castle. George cut off the dragon's head in front of all of the villagers.

The Eastern Dragon: A Magical Friend

Eastern dragons are very different from their Western cousins. They have power over nature. Eastern dragons have the ability to change the seasons. They can control seas, lakes, and rivers. They can also create clouds by breathing. When upset, Eastern dragons can use their powers to cause natural disasters, such as floods and hurricanes.

In many Eastern stories, a dragon can shape-shift. It often appears as a wise old man or a beautiful young woman. In ancient China, the emperor was

Eastern dragons are known for being wise and kind.

known as the dragon. For more than 4,000 years, dragons have held a place of honor in East Asian cultures.

The Legend of the Four Dragons

One Eastern legend explains how dragons formed China's four great rivers. Four dragons lived in the Eastern Sea—the black dragon, the long dragon, the pearl dragon, and the yellow dragon. China did not have any rivers. The land was very dry. People needed rain to grow their crops. One year, the rain stopped falling. All the crops died. Without crops for food, the people began to starve.

The four dragons decided to help China's people. They scooped water from the sea and sprayed it into the sky. The water fell as if it were rain. The crops soaked up the water and grew again.

The god of the sea was angry at the dragons. They had taken his water without asking permission. He told China's emperor the dragons had stolen from him. The emperor

Gift of Writing

In one Eastern legend, a dragon-horse with scales and wings rose from the Lo River around the year 2960 BCE. Black marks decorated the dragon's back. The Chinese Emperor Fu Hsi saw the dragon and its strange markings. He drew the marks from the dragon's back, and they became the eight primary characters of the Chinese written language. The dragon had shared the secret of writing with Fu Hsi. The emperor then shared the dragon's gift with the Chinese people.

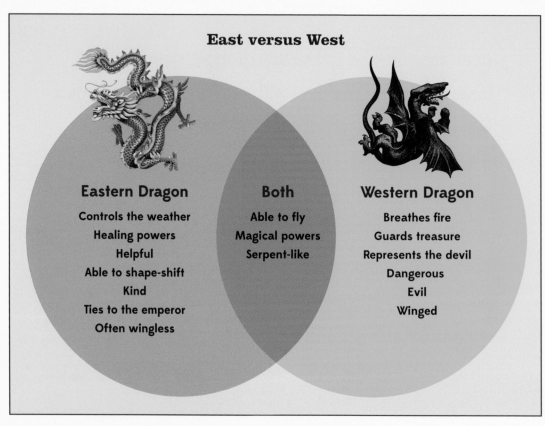

East versus West

Eastern Dragon

Controls the weather
Healing powers
Helpful
Able to shape-shift
Kind
Ties to the emperor
Often wingless

Both

Able to fly
Magical powers
Serpent-like

Western Dragon

Breathes fire
Guards treasure
Represents the devil
Dangerous
Evil
Winged

Eastern and Western Dragons

This diagram compares some of the main features of Eastern and Western dragons. What features do both dragons share? What other features could you add to this diagram?

punished the dragons and put them in prison under four mountains. To help the people, the dragons turned themselves into four rivers—the Black River, the Long River, The Pearl River, and the Yellow River. These rivers brought the water the people needed.

Other Dragons

Dragon mythology is a part of cultures outside of Europe and Asia too. In North America and South America, some modern stories tell of the *amphithere*. The amphithere is a large flying dragon. Its only limbs are its set of wings. In Australia ancient rock art shows a dragon-like creature known as a rainbow serpent. Some of the drawings show a snake-like creature with a kangaroo's head and a crocodile's tail.

CHAPTER FIVE

DRAGONS TODAY

Few people today believe dragons exist. But these exciting creatures are still important in cultures around the world. Today dragon mythology has a special place in popular media, such as books and movies.

Dragons in Books

Some of the most famous dragons in pop culture are characters in well-loved books. Smaug is a

In the 2010 film *How to Train Your Dragon*, Toothless is a friendly dragon that becomes friends with a Viking boy.

fire-breathing dragon from J. R. R. Tolkien's *The Hobbit*, published in 1937. Smaug flies through the sky. He controls people with his voice and eyes. Smaug also guards a large treasure in a mountain cave.

Dangerous dragons are part of the Harry Potter books by author J. K. Rowling. The Harry Potter series was published between 1997 and 2007. There are many types of dragons in Rowling's books. Like many Western dragons, some of Rowling's dragons guard treasure.

Basilisk

In *Harry Potter and the Chamber of Secrets*, a basilisk threatens Hogwarts, Harry Potter's school. The basilisk is a creature based on European legends from nearly 2,000 years ago. According to legend, a basilisk is a dragon-like creature. It looks like a giant snake or lizard. In some myths, the basilisk could kill its victims with a single glance. In the Harry Potter book and movie, the beast paralyzes anyone who sees it indirectly, such as in a mirror. Anyone who sees the basilisk directly is killed instantly.

In the film Harry Potter and the Chamber of Secrets, Harry finds the skin of a dragon-like basilisk that threatens his school.

The Big Screen

Dragons have also soared into movies. Some films are based on books. Films based on the Harry Potter series were released between 2001 and 2011. The first film in a three-movie adaptation of *The Hobbit* was released in 2012.

Bringing a dragon to life in a movie is a challenge. Some filmmakers create dragons as cartoon characters. The dragons in 1998's *Mulan* and 2001's *Shrek* are drawn as cartoons. Other films have lifelike dragons made by computer-generated images (CGI).

CGI can make movie dragons seem almost as real as the human actors in a film.

The dragon Saphira starred in *Eragon*, a movie released in 2006. The film is based on the book by Christopher Paolini. Filmmakers used CGI to create Saphira. They gave her blue scales, two horns, and a powerful spiked tail. To make Saphira fly, filmmakers studied the way eagles fly. Many moviegoers praised the realistic movie dragon.

The Softer Side of Dragons

As in ancient dragon mythology, many movie dragons are friendly. These dragons are often drawn as funny cartoon characters. In 2010 DreamWorks Animation released *How to Train Your Dragon*. The film is based on a book by author Cressida Crowell. In the movie, dragons fly over a mythical Viking village. Young Viking boys prove their bravery by killing dragons. In the film, Hiccup is a Viking who shoots down a flying dragon during a battle. He decides to set the dragon free instead of killing it. The boy and the dragon,

CGI was used to create the realistic-looking dragons in the film *Eragon*.

The Chinese Dragon Dance

Chinese New Year is one of the most important holidays in China and its neighboring countries. Dragons are an important part of the celebration. During the Chinese New Year celebration, dancers carry brightly colored dragon forms on poles in large parades down city streets. One dancer moves the dragon's head. The others move its body. Music from drums, cymbals, and gongs keeps the beat as the dragon moves. Chinese tradition says the longer the dragon's body, the more luck it will bring.

named Toothless, become friends. Eventually, Hiccup and Toothless work together to save dragons and humans from an evil dragon.

Dragons have been popular for thousands of years. They have played important roles in ancient myths and blockbuster movies alike. Legendary dragons will surely entertain people for centuries to come.

The dragon dance is used to celebrate the New Year in many Eastern countries.

Asian Lung

China

In Eastern art and stories, the lung flies without wings. Often, it carries a large magic pearl, which gives it the ability to fly. It has long, whisker-like feelers and a mane. It is often found near water.

Rainbow Serpent

Australia

Ancient rock art from more than 6,000 years ago shows the snake-like Rainbow Serpent. In some art, the creature has a kangaroo's head and a crocodile's tail. It has power over rains, storms, and floods.

European Dragon

Europe

Pictures of the European dragon often show it breathing fire. It loves treasure and usually makes its home in a mountain or sea cave. It has a barbed tail and large, bat-like wings.

Fafnir

Scandinavia

Fafnir is a dragon from a Scandinavian story. He is covered in scales and guards a treasure. According to the legend of Fafnir, anyone who eats the heart of a dragon will have the ability to understand the speech of birds.

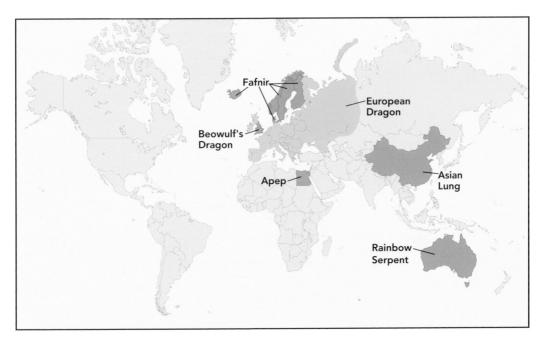

Beowulf's Dragon

England

According to an Anglo-Saxon poem from approximately 700 CE, this is a fierce flying dragon that breathes fire and guards a treasure. Its body is covered by tough scales, except for its belly, which is unprotected.

Apep

Egypt

This dragon was an ancient Egyptian god who wanted to eat the sun. In early legends, Apep is described as a large snake-like creature. Some legends say he is nearly 50 feet (15 m) long.

Why Do I Care?

Some dragon legends date back thousands of years. See if you can find any similarities between your life and ancient legends. What parts of your life could you explain with a modern legend? How would you pass on your legend to future generations? What changes might occur to the legend over time? Use your imagination!

Take a Stand

This book discusses different ways dragon legends may have formed. Which explanations in the book seem the most believable to you? Write a short essay explaining your opinion. Make sure to give reasons for your opinion and facts and details to support those reasons.

Say What?

Studying dragon legends can mean learning many new words. Find five words in this book you have never read before. Use a dictionary to find out what they mean. Then write the meanings in your own words, and use each word in a new sentence.

You Are There

This book discusses how people may have reacted to seeing new and unusual animals. Imagine you are traveling to an exotic place for the first time. Suddenly, you see a terrifying creature you have never seen before. How will you describe it? What stories will you tell about it?

GLOSSARY

Anglo-Saxons
people who took over
England in the 400s CE

cryptozoologist
a person who studies
creatures that have not been
proven to exist by modern
science

culture
a way of life, customs, and
traditions shared among a
group of people

fossil
the remains of an animal or
plant from millions of years
ago, preserved in rock

lair
a place where a wild animal
sleeps and rests

Middle Ages
a period of European history
ranging from approximately
the 400s to the 1400s CE

paralyze
to make something helpless
or unable to move

reptile
a cold-blooded animal that
crawls across the ground or
uses short legs

sacrifice
to give up something
precious for an important
reason

vulnerable
able to be hurt

LEARN MORE

Books

Cain, Patrick. *Komodo Dragon*. Minneapolis: ABDO, 2014.

Drake, Ernest. *Drake's Comprehensive Compendium of Dragonology*. Boston: Candlewick, 2009.

Rumford, James. *Beowulf: A Hero's Tale Retold*. New York: Houghton Mifflin, 2007.

Web Links

To learn more about dragons, visit ABDO Publishing Company online at **www.abdopublishing.com**. Web sites about dragons are featured on our Book Links page. These links are routinely monitored and updated to provide the most current information available.

Visit **www.mycorelibrary.com** for free additional tools for teachers and students.

INDEX

ABOUT THE AUTHOR

Carla Mooney is the author of several books for young readers. A graduate of the University of Pennsylvania, she lives in Pittsburgh, Pennsylvania, with her husband and three children.

DATE DUE

PRINTED IN U.S.A.